T0132266

Mommy, why do we take baths?

By

Jennifer Smith

© Copyright 2019 Jennifer Smith.

All rights reserved. No part of this publication may be reproduced, stored in a retrieval system, or transmitted, in any form or by any means, electronic, mechanical, photocopying, recording, or otherwise, without the written prior permission of the author.

Order this book online at www.trafford.com
or email orders@trafford.com

Most Trafford titles are also available at major online book retailers.

 www.trafford.com

North America & international
toll-free: 1 888 232 4444 (USA & Canada)
fax: 812 355 4082

Our mission is to efficiently provide the world's finest, most comprehensive book publishing service, enabling every author to experience success. To find out how to publish your book, your way, and have it available worldwide, visit us online at www.trafford.com

Because of the dynamic nature of the Internet, any web addresses or links contained in this book may have changed since publication and may no longer be valid. The views expressed in this work are solely those of the author and do not necessarily reflect the views of the publisher, and the publisher hereby disclaims any responsibility for them.

Any people depicted in stock imagery provided by Getty Images are models, and such images are being used for illustrative purposes only.
Certain stock imagery © Getty Images.
ISBN: 978-1-4907-9736-6 (sc)
ISBN: 978-1-4907-9737-3 (hc)
ISBN: 978-1-4907-9735-9 (e)

Print information available on the last page.

Trafford rev. 09/17/2019

Dedicated to

Jabari and Jordan

MOMMY SAYS THAT WE SHOULD TAKE BATHS BECAUSE THEY HELP US GET THE DIRT FROM THE DAY OFF OF OUR BODIES.

"Ewwwwww, dirt! We get dirty from the park and playing outside!

MOMMY RUNS MY WARM BATH WATER
AND ADDS BUBBLES.

"Yaaaaaay bubbles! Bubbles
are fun!"

MOMMY CLEANS MY FACE AND WASHES MY HEAD TO GET THE DIRT OFF.

"Weeeee! !"

MOMMY CLEANS ME ALL OVER WITH
SOAP AND A WASH CLOTH.

MOMMY CLEANS MY EARS...

AND WASHES MY BODY, HANDS,
FINGERS, FEET AND TOES.

AND THE BEST PART IS, MOMMY
TALKS TO ME AND ASKS ME ABOUT
MY DAY.

WHEN MY MOMMY IS DONE WASHING ME SHE TAKES ME OUT OF THE TUB AND DRIES ME OFF.

THEN MY MOMMY GIVES ME A BABY MASSAGE WITH LOTION AND PUTS MY JAMMIES ON.

THEN MOMMY BRUSHES MY HAIR.

NOW, I CAN GO TO SLEEP CLEAN
AND HAVE SWEET DREAMS.

"Night! Night!"

Printed in the United States
By Bookmasters